BRANDON COBB

10 Simple Habits to Improve Your Life

Small Changes You Can Make Today To Create A Better Tomorrow

Disclaimer

The material in this publication is of the nature of general comment only, and does not represent professional advice. It is not intended to provide specific guidance for particular circumstances and it should not be relied on as the basis for any decision to take action or not take action on any matter which it covers. Readers should obtain professional advice where appropriate, before making any such decision. To the maximum extent permitted by law, the author and publisher disclaim all responsibility and liability to any person, arising directly or indirectly from any person taking or not taking action based on the information in this publication.

First edition

This book was professionally typeset on Reedsy.
Find out more at reedsy.com

Contents

Introduction

Habits. There are good ones, and there are - *not so good ones.*

The Merriam-Webster dictionary defines a habit as "An acquired mode of behavior that has become nearly or completely involuntary," and additionally, "A behavior pattern acquired by frequent repetition or physiologic exposure that shows itself in regularity or increased facility of performance."

Some habits can be trained; focusing on steps to deliberately develop a pattern of action or behavior that will eventually take on an almost automated function, while other habits are developed naturally over the course of one's life; whether intentional or not, such as nail biting, for example. Sometimes the best intentions are interrupted by a tendency to continue, or to fall into, or to fall *back* into, a negative habit. Likewise, sometimes things such as poor behavior, a negative outlook, a weakness in one's physical, social, psychological, or professional life, can be altered; changed for the better just by analyzing the various habits that we have developed over time, then focusing on the those that help us, eliminating the ones that do not serve us, and creating new ones that will help move us forward and grow. We all have the ability within us to make the changes necessary to positively impact our lives.

How long will it take? Well, if you do an internet search for the length of time it takes to develop and solidify a new habit, you will surely find varying opinions. One suggestion that is frequently referenced is twenty-one days, though this number may have been sourced from dated literature that has since made its way into common thought. Some suggest it could be anywhere between two weeks and two-hundred days, and yet more recent research suggests it's closer to around sixty days. Ultimately, it really just depends on the habit you are trying to create, the type of person you are, the circumstances in your life, and where exactly you wish to see yourself and what obstacles might stand in your way.

The good news is, no matter how long it may take to solidify the habit, it takes no time to actually begin working on it. It only requires the decision to do so, and the action of taking the first step. The act of deciding alone is already a move in the right direction and when you begin to move on that decision, you will begin to positively impact your life. One good habit will often lead to another, and then more positive things are sure to follow!

If you don't know where to begin on this journey of good habits or you are just looking for an easy way to make quick positive changes, then please allow this book to provide you with a list of simple actions that you can begin today in order to better improve your tomorrow.

Good Luck!

1

USE YOUR CALENDAR

You may have heard the saying "Time is relative," or that "Time is a construct," and wouldn't it be nice if we could wake and sleep only when our bodies felt like it, or go to work whenever we wished, or expect the theater to play the movie we want to see when it fits our mood, and not when *they* decide to set the showtimes. This of course is not how the world works, and that's not necessarily a bad thing.

Humans noticed a long time ago that the sun appeared to rise and fall in a pattern and they figured out a way to measure it and to keep track of it. As such, people were better able to map out their future — whether it be when to plant crops, when the next train will arrive, determining how long it would take to design and build a structure, when to take a coffee break, or when to host their child's next birthday party. The ability to track and schedule tasks and events on a uniformly used tool {The Calendar} is one of the many things that has pushed societies into the future and helped them to advance civilization.

One of the great things about a calendar is that you can use it to schedule just about anything - including your positive habits. Have an exercise routine? Put it on the calendar. Need to be at a meeting by 9:00 on Tuesday? Put it on the calendar. Need to remember to buy your spouse an anniversary gift? You already guessed it... Put it on the calendar. Although there have been variations over the centuries, such as the famous Mayan calendar, and still other forms of calendars observed to this day, such as the Chinese calendar, for this section and ease of concept, we'll assume that everyone agrees to use the standard Gregorian calendar.

And unless we decide to re-measure how we view time, we each have 365 days a year; every year (except for those wacky leap years of course). And wouldn't you know, every person on the planet gets the same 365 days on their calendar as you do. The same goes for the number of weeks in a year, the number of days in a week, the number of hours in a day, and so on. Do you ever wonder how some people are able to accomplish so much and then wonder where they found the time? How is it that two people can share the same day, yet one person can run a billion-dollar corporation while the other can barely find the time to fold their socks. The answer may simply lie within Time Management. They utilize their calendar. They have a schedule. And they stick to it.

Luckily, there are many options available to aid in this habit. For those that prefer the standard paper method, there are small calendars that fit nicely in the corner of your desk that you may glance at, or giant desk calendars which act as a place mat in which you work on top of, all the while looking directly at your days on the page, wall calendars, pocket calendars, reminder books, and the oh so helpful day-planner, which is very popular for the professional and for the super organized person.

Many planners offer inserts that can be ordered and replenished for each new year — this is often beneficial in that you can keep many of the commonly used pages, such as passwords, addresses, phone numbers, etc. in the planner and just replace the month/week pages when needed. Some paper planners have open date fields and just continuous pages of empty days of which you can manually write in the appropriate month/date, while others can be purchased with the current year's dates already provided. Additionally, most planners provide a page for the entire month, which will give you a broad view of any important tasks to prepare for or look forward to, as well as separate pages for each of the weeks that fall within a particular month so that you may focus on more immediate priorities or events.

You may also find several options that provide areas for note taking, for goal setting, for important dates, and there are even those that aim to assist you in your growth throughout the year, such as practicing daily gratitude by providing sections to enter what your are grateful for each day or week, or listing your accomplishments, or providing check-boxes to track your water intake for the day. Often times these planners will also have colored tabs that you can attach as needed to help you segment out each month or flag important events. Whatever you are looking for in a paper calendar, you will likely find a useful product out there that will provide just what you need in order to manage your life.

Of course, if you're the type that finds using paper to be cumbersome — having to carry your planner between locations, or you find pen to paper to be too time consuming or boring, or perhaps it's just difficult to remember to look at your calendar each day and you're the type of person that just prefers a more modern tool for tracking and planning your schedule, there is of course an electronic version.

Not too long ago, (but before smartphones were widely used), there were Personal Digital Assistants — think Palm Pilot — handheld devices that acted as a calculator, a calendar, a Rolodex, and even a way to sign documents. Then as time went on, we see Blackberry phones that could also send and receive emails, and then of course you move further into the current age of handheld devices, of which nearly everyone on the street now has one in their pocket, and they can not only do everything the predecessors were capable of, but can do more than ever dreamed of even 20 years prior. Now, fast forward to today and the newest smart*Watches* currently on the market have more computing power than the first smart*Phones* once did. Why is this relevant? Because now you can have a calendar right on your wrist, and this calendar can connect seamlessly with your phone calendar, your computer's desktop calendar, and even be shared amongst family and colleagues.

It isn't just your basic calendar anymore either; advancements in technology have allowed for several applications and functionality to be developed that will help to keep you on track with reminders, alerts, and automated scheduling, such as calculating driving times for you when you have appointments or meetings to attend. Everything that can be performed on paper can now be performed digitally, with greater efficacy, and with ease.

So, what goes on a calendar? Well, everything — or rather, everything of relative importance that is. This can include things such as tasks, deadlines, important dates, memorable occasions, short term or long term goals, bills due, and any accomplishments you wish to complete. And don't forget to include the fun stuff too, like date night and your family vacations!

List your goals and then break them up by distance. 5 years, 1 year, 1 month, 1 week, 1 day, and hourly, then work backwards.

Though five years may seem like a long way from now, it will surely come. Being able to identify where you wish to be at that time and then writing this down will help to bring those desires into existence. The mere act of putting it on paper (or electronic paper) begins the process of achieving those goals. For your five year plan, write out in detail the things you wish to do by then; the places you wish to go, the house, car, job, skill, etc. that you wish to acquire and then save this information somewhere that you can view it often. So that you are constantly reminded of what you are working towards; a great place would be the notes or goals page of your planner or as the wallpaper on your smartphone!

For your one year entries, be sure to include anything that is necessary during that year which will help you to move closer toward your five year goals, then place any other dates of importance on your calendar as well.

For your one month entries, look forward to the next thirty days and determine any appointments, anniversaries, due dates, etc. and enter those into the broad calendar area.

Likewise, your weeks should be designed to follow your important monthly dates, with the addition of weekly tasks or goals, such as Monday = Gym, Wednesday = Clean Garage.

Following suite, your individual days should naturally follow your week with the addition of an hourly breakdown, i.e.
06:00 - Wake
07:00 - Exercise

09:00 - Work
12:00 - Lunch

Ultimately, the calendar is just a visual tool that allows you to view your day-to-day and see down the road in order prioritize and meet your goals and needs in a way that keeps you organized, efficient, and progressing towards positive growth. Use this tool in congruence with your alarm clock, with your reminder applications, and with your watch in order to ensure that you remain task oriented and that you are consistently moving forward.

The calendar is your friend.

2

WAKE UP EARLY

Maybe you remember the famous quote by Benjamin Franklin, "Early to bed and early to rise makes a man healthy, wealthy, and wise," and there is a reason this individual stands out as one of our wisest historical influencers — because that's just sound advice!

Getting proper sleep is one of the greatest things you can do to positively affect your physical and mental well-being. Sleep shouldn't be sacrificed if you can help it, but it also should not be overdone either. Strive to acquire 7 to 8 hours of decent solid sleep each night so that you don't incur a sleep debt and so that your mind and body can heal and re-energize and truly absorb the benefits of receiving a good night's sleep. But, assuming you are receiving the proper amount of sleep as needed, set a schedule around this that will allow you to wake up early in the morning (or for those night-shifters, early in the evening), and reap the additional benefits of having this extra time to focus on your goals and positive habits.

Decide on a crisp early morning hour to wake and subtract 7 to 8 hours to know when you should go to bed each night. Make this your routine. Mark it on your calendar. Set your alarm and begin training your internal clock to live on this schedule. At first, you may find it difficult, but just like anything else, the more you do it, the easier it becomes. Soon, you may discover that you don't even need an alarm clock and your body will naturally wake to this rhythm.

There is a sense of peace in the air on early morning days. The sun is slow to ease into the sky, the house is quiet, the fresh cup of coffee tends to smell and taste just a little better, and you can have this time to yourself, alone with just your thoughts and your breath. Early mornings are themselves a small sanctuary. Enjoy them. Appreciate them. Take advantage of what they have to offer.

Use this time to relax briefly before you begin your day, but don't let it fully slip away — this is also an opportunity to do the tasks or perform the habits you wish to accomplish that the hustle and bustle of your active day may not allow. This could be meditating, folding laundry, studying, reviewing your calendar, exercising, reading, taking the dog for a walk, doing the dishes from the night before, or simply pondering about the things you are grateful for (a very positive habit).

Anything that you would normally struggle to fit into your daily schedule, see if you can fit it into a morning routine. You will feel accomplished before your day even truly begins and if you run into obstacles later on or find that your day has just simply gotten away from you; unexpected meetings, calls from the school to pick up your kid, car suddenly needs a new tire, etc., then you can at still appreciate the fact that you were able to accomplish *something* that day; it wasn't a complete waste and you can be grateful that you at least had that precious quiet morning and can look forward to the next one. You may find that the stresses of your days aren't as bad as they had once seemed.

3

MAKE YOUR BED

Making your bed may have always been a tedious task that your parents harped on you to do each day, but it certainly doesn't have to be that way now.

It might seem like a silly thing to consider as being an important habit, but it is one of the simplest things that you can perform which provides much satisfaction and perhaps an unknowing benefit to your life.

If you sleep alone, enthusiastically throw the pillows to the side and toss the blankets into the air and watch them float back down, pull, fold, tuck, fluff until it looks properly made, then stand back for a moment and appreciate the clean and tidy appearance and feel good about getting something done before you even begin your day. If you sleep with a spouse or partner that doesn't wake during the same time you do, feel free to wait until you are both awake and as a team make it a habit to return the shuffled blankets and pillows to their pre-slept in state. It can be a positive action that you can share with your loved one. If they do not wake before you are ready to leave or start your morning, at least quietly tidy up your side of the bed, but ultimately, the goal is to leave your place of slumber neatly fluffed, folded, and tucked away before you truly begin your day.

If you make this the first habit that you do when you wake, the action of moving about while making your bed will begin to get the blood flowing in your body and increase the oxygen intake to your brain. This helps to wake the body and mind further, which makes early morning grogginess less noticeable.

It isn't merely a physical benefit, however; your mental well-being is also positively affected. You literally begin your day with a small accomplishment. This is a psychological hack. It creates positive feedback and begins to program your mind to want to do more actions that will lead to feelings of accomplishment. Not to mention, if nothing else were to go right throughout your day, for example, if you were bombarded with deadlines, phone calls, or one unscheduled task after another, or visited by well-meaning friends or family that overstayed and prevented you from accomplishing anything else you set out to do, you can still take solace in the fact that you at least completed **Something**, and when you are exhausted and ready to collapse from your long day, that *something* will be waiting for you, looking crisp and comfy and inviting. It always feels better to sleep in a freshly made bed.

So remember what your mama told you, *"Make your bed."*

4

DRINK WATER

This may sound like a basic concept, but, just like the previous habits mentioned, it's often the simplest acts that can provide some of the greatest benefits.

Your body, as we all know, is made up of a significant amount of water; roughly 60% on average, (depending on which research you follow), but even though the number can vary due to things like age, sex, and hydration levels, the approximate volume is typically going to fall within this percentage.

Without these amazing molecules, your system would cease to function. Your body is an incredible organic machine, and just like most machines, you must ensure the required fuels are put into it in order to keep it functioning properly. Every part of your body utilizes water, so it is important that before any other additives are put into it, water should be number one on the list.

Here are just a few things in your body that water is used for:

- Regulating Body Temperature
- Lubricating/Cushioning Joints
- Waste Removal (sweat, urine, bowl movements)
- Carries Oxygen to the Cells
- Transports Nutrients Through the Body
- Helps to Maintain Electrolyte Balance
- Helps to Digest Food

The list goes on, but the key thing to take away from this is that you need water, and it is important that you provide yourself with a sufficient amount in order for your body and mind to function properly and at their highest level.

Disclaimer: There is such thing as drinking too much water. Which can lead to serious issues, like over-hydration. When one is over-hydrated, they might experience minor symptoms, such as headaches, drowsiness or confusion, but it can also become worse and cause issues like disruption of brain function, high blood pressure, electrolyte imbalance, and low heart rate. So, just as the old saying goes — *Everything in moderation!*

Don't let this frighten you, however; you still need water. The issue with most people is that they aren't receiving as much as they should and instead of choosing good'ol H2O, often times their bodies are being provided with less than healthy alternatives, such as alcohol, sugary soft drinks, high levels of caffeine in the form of energy drinks or more cups of coffee than are really needed. Most of these alternative beverages also come along with the unfortunate drawbacks of unwanted calories, dyes, additives, chemicals, sugars, and the extra financial costs. Sure, they taste great and they make you feel some type of way, but ultimately, choosing these products over a simple glass of water can eventually cause more trouble than it's worth.

If you need an exact number of how much to drink, the usual guidelines have been 6-8 glasses a day, depending on your activity level, body type, and personal needs of course — but this is a good standard for most.

Basically, follow these simple rules: drink [water] when you are thirsty; drink more when you are performing physical exercise or sweating more; a nice big glass first thing in the morning is a good way to begin your day; don't overdue it; and if you can replace at least one cup of coffee or a soft drink with a bottle of water, then try to do so. Your body will thank you.

5

DIET & EXERCISE

This is technically two habits combined into one, but that is because diet and exercise go hand-in-hand. One without the other is only half the pie… or perhaps "Pie" is the wrong term to use — Half of the puzzle!

You can exercise seven days per week, yet if you eat like absolute garbage, your results will be hardly noticeable. You would have to increase your performance at the gym considerably in order to balance the effects of a poor diet. Likewise, you can eat the healthiest diet on earth, yet if you live a sedentary lifestyle, never using your body, never working your heart and lungs and moving your muscles, you are still doing your body a disservice.

You were designed to move and your brain, organs, and cells all thrive when they are worked as intended. Lethargy breeds more lethargy. You've likely heard the notion, "A body in motion, stays in motion; a body at rest, stays at rest." If you don't use your body, your body will be of no use.

Thousands of books and programs have been developed and promoted covering these topics, all sharing systems, ideas, plans, routines, and advice. Depending on a multitude of factors, such as age, sex, health, body type, goals, and so forth, you can search through a plethora of data that would be best suited for you, and you might also get lost in the vast ocean of available options. So, how can we make things a little easier for the purpose of this section? — It all comes down to choices.

That's probably the simplest way to begin working towards the best course of action when it comes to diet and exercise, anyway; it's the choices you make. This can begin with baby steps; small changes that eventually lead into bigger changes. Let's say you're a big fan of fast food restaurants. First baby step — "Today, I'm not going to super-size my meal." Next baby step — "I think I'll have a bottled water with my meal instead of a soft drink." Next baby step — "Ya' know, I think I might try making my own lunch today." And so on and so forth.

<u>Quick rules of thumb</u>: Choose less processed over processed. Choose natural sweets over sugar. Choose water, juice, tea over sodas, alcohol, energy drinks. Choose fruits, vegetables, nuts, berries, seeds, and lean proteins over candy, cakes, deep fried anything, and fast food burgers. Choose frozen yogurt over ice-cream. Choose whole-grain bread over white-bread. You get the picture.

You'll begin to feel good about making the better choices, and then one good choice will start a cascade of better choices down the road. Soon you may discover that your refrigerator is filled with more vegetables than before, your snacks consist of more fruits and nuts, your dinners are filled with more healthy proteins and less carbs and heavy starches. Your diet is becoming more nutrient dense, less processed, and more satiating and satisfying.

It is no different when it comes to exercise. There's always going to be options. "Should I take the elevator or the stairs?" "Should I look for the closest parking spot or park some distance away and get those extra steps in?" "Should I go to the gym after work or go see a movie?" "Should I play this video game or should I take the dog out for a walk?"

Once you get into the habit of taking the path of more resistance, your mind begins reprogramming. You find satisfaction in the challenge. The mind and body respond positively to healthy stress and become stronger by it. Soon you will find that exercise is not only much needed, but much desired. Set small goals that are easily attainable, but not so easy that you have no hurdles to climb over; you need the challenge. When you reach these goals, you will see a desire to accomplish even greater goals.

One easily attainable, yet challenging goal is to walk each day. Walking not only exercises the cardiovascular system, but it is low impact on your knees, which is great for those who are unable to jog due to painful joints. Walking is also a great mood booster, especially if you can do it outside where you can breathe in the fresh air and absorb sunlight. If your job allows small breaks during the day, choose to go on a brief walk rather than sitting at your desk or in a break-room staring at your phone. Walking can also ease mental and physical stress and even help you with decision making and problem solving. If you have a spouse or partner or children, try to invite them to join you on your walks and use it as quality time together (unless of course you prefer the solitude that a private walk can provide; which is great as well!). Though don't forget to consider inviting your K-9 companion to come along should you have one; it will often be the highlight of their day.

Another way of creating small hurdles is to build yourself small non-negotiable routines. For instance, each day, *no matter what,* you must do three simple sets of exercises, such as push-ups, sit-ups, and squats. (This is just a suggestion of course; you may certainly use this idea or create your own set of exercises), but going with this example, you would set the number of reps to something that is challenging, but not impossible; say 20 reps for each exercise (or set to your own abilities). Then, no matter the time of day, how you feel, what has come up, there is no negotiating with yourself. No, "I'll just do it tomorrow," or "Missing one day won't hurt." Because missing one day *Will* hurt. It creates a break in momentum and it tells your brain that it's OK to not be dedicated to this change, and making a habit requires repeated consistent action. If your entire day has been a flurry of busyness and you are finally lying in bed and you realize that you haven't performed your non-negotiables, then you *must* jump out of bed and knock them out. Even if it means doing sit-ups in your pajamas at 10:00 at night.

This type of dedication will prove something to yourself — that you are the type of person who can commit and you choose to have positive healthy habits over lazy habits. Something else you may notice when you perform these small non-negotiable exercises, is that some days you might feel a little extra energized by them and may decide to throw in another set or two. Of course, do not limit yourself to only these few things each day. Certainly set up a regular exercise plan if you have the time and ability, but keep these non-negotiables in your pocket, because if for any reason you are unable to reach your scheduled goals for that day, you know that you still have these to fall back on and the day was not a total miss.

Quick Rules of Thumb: Try to get a balance of both cardio and resistance training. Strive for at least 20 minutes of dedicated exercise at least 3 days per week (but don't forget about those non-negotiables in your pocket). It's always recommended to consult a medical professional before beginning any type of routine or plan. Know your limits, but don't be afraid to push the boundaries (stress = growth). Remember to stretch. Flexibility is taken for granted when we are young. Regular stretching and flexibility training will help to prevent many injuries, especially as you get older. And remind yourself that short-term pain leads to long-term pleasure, but if you settle for the short-term pleasure instead, then you risk the long-term pain down the road.

6

MEDITATION

Breath in…. Breath out…. Repeat

Just breathe. On the one hand, meditation is as simple as that. On the other hand, there are many ways to meditate and no single style that works for everyone. But with practice, patience, and a desire to be *in the present moment*, anyone can find the method that works best for them and begin receiving the many benefits that meditation can provide.

What kind of benefits? Well, here are some of the things you might expect:

- Reduces Stress
- Improves Concentration
- Reduces Anxiety
- Reduces Depression
- Improves Sleep
- Lowers Blood Pressure
- Boosts the Immune System

- Helps to Manage Pain
- Promotes a Sense of Well-Being
- Improves Cognitive Function

There are scientifically proven mental and physical health benefits that are gained from regular meditation practice. For many, however, the idea of sitting quietly in an odd pose and doing nothing for minutes on end might sound strange or silly or *boring*, but it is this state of boredom that you are looking for. You want to remove yourself from all of the activities of the day, the worry of tomorrow, the thoughts of the past. During meditation, you strive to be in the present moment, alone with your breath, with your inner self.

But meditating doesn't have to strictly be candles lit, lotus pose, incense burning, and singing bowls chiming in background. Meditation can be performed anywhere at any time. You can meditate on the subway on your way to work. You can meditate on your porch swing overlooking your yard. You can meditate at your desk during a short break. You can meditate while you take an evening walk or while you're soaking in the bathtub.

The point is, no one should say they never have time to dedicate to meditation practice; it's free, it can be done anywhere, and it is within you to do so always.

Just like everything else, start off small and work your way up. You will most surely find it difficult to quiet your mind, initially, (referred to as the "Monkey Mind" in Buddhist meditation), but with consistent practice, you will find it easier to enter a meditative state, and as time passes, you will begin to look forward to these moments with yourself.

Try scheduling a block of time each day to practice your meditation — early mornings are a good time to dedicate to it. It is typically quieter in the mornings, and often times you will have moments to yourself (if you are waking before others) and just like your other morning habits, you begin the day with an accomplishment which sets the pace for the rest of the day. If you are an experienced meditator, then certainly schedule in the amount of time that you feel comfortable with, but for those just beginning the practice, do not attempt to push 20 to 30 minutes or an hour of meditation; this is too much for someone just starting out. Try small blocks; 1 minute every morning of simply sitting quietly with your eyes closed and just following slow deep breaths in and out of your diaphragm. Give this a few days and then try increasing the amount of time; push it to 5 minutes. Do this for at least a week or until you feel comfortable moving beyond it. Then as you have begun to get in the groove of the process, see how long you can sit in this focused, relaxing state of calm.

There are numerous books, websites, and applications that are designed to help people with their meditation journey, from relaxing sounds, to guided sessions, to education on the different forms and styles of meditation. There are even live classes that you can attend. Whatever your needs are, there is something for everyone.

If you would like a quick and easy to follow guide for a general beginner meditation, feel free to try the steps below to get you started:

- Find a quiet place that you know will be free of distractions for the amount of time you wish to set aside; let's say 1 - 5 minutes. (Shut off your phone or leave it somewhere else as to not receive any unexpected interruptions, unless you are using a meditation app, in which case turn on airplane mode).

- Dim the lights or close the curtains if possible, to set a relaxing atmosphere.

- If you'd like, find some soft music or calming white noise. This can be things like nature sounds, such as ocean waves, a river stream, rainfall, (sounds of water can be very relaxing), birds chirping, fire crackling — or perhaps you'd prefer soothing instruments, like a gentle harp or maybe some new-aged music, such as lo-fi beats. Or go the traditional route and play Tibetan bowls or Buddhist chanting. Some people do better with total silence while others find the ambient sounds to aid in their process.

- Find a comfortable place to sit or lie down. You don't have to have a special meditation pillow or incense burning unless you want to, but it does help to create a unique place of relaxation where you know the intentions of this space are to calm yourself and focus on the present moment.

- You can experiment with different postures until you find one that works best for you. The important thing is to be comfortable, but not so comfortable that you are going to drift off to sleep — So maybe don't meditate in bed unless you are using it for the intended purpose of falling asleep easier.

- Once you are ready to begin, use a timer or set an alarm on your watch, or press start on an app if you are using one and then:

1. Gently close your eyes

— You don't have to squeeze them shut to ensure they are completely sealed, but just relax them enough to allow them to softly close; even leaving them hazily open if necessary.

2. Take a long deep breath through your nose.

— It will help if you try to visualize bright healing light being inhaled as you do so.

— As you breathe in, count this breath for approximately 3 to 5 seconds, then hold for approximately 5 to 8 seconds.

— Then breathe out slowly through your mouth for approximately 8 to 10 seconds and visualize a different color light exiting your body, which is now carrying away stress and contaminants and negative energy as it leaves.

3. Continue this process for 3 to 5 rounds while focusing your attention on nothing but the breath and the count.

— **In**, 1,2,3,4, **Hold**, 1,2,3,4,5,6,7, **Out**, 1,2,3,4,5,6,7,8,9, **Repeat**.

4. After doing this a few times, allow your breathing to slowly return to normal and don't try to control it; only watch it.

— Feel the breath as it enters your lungs; feel your chest and diaphragm rise and fall. Scan your body. Notice any sensations you are having; the feeling of the floor or chair beneath you; the breeze of a fan on your face; the subtle beating of your pulse.

— Notice and acknowledge these sensations; let any sounds, smells, or feelings aid in your relaxation. They are there to help calm you. And just breathe.

5. If you find yourself distracted; your thoughts beginning to trail off, simply return to the breath and say to yourself "In…" "Out…" "In…" "Out…" as you do.

6. Know that it is OK for your mind to drift; this is perfectly natural and happens to everyone, even the most experienced meditators. The important thing is to acknowledge it and let the thoughts pass on by, then return back to the breath. You may do this a thousand times, but each time builds strength and eventually the act will feel effortless.

7. Your goal is not to achieve anything in this moment. It is not to solve any issues or gain any type of perspective. It is simply to be. To be in the present moment.

8. After your meditation is complete, evaluate how you feel. Better? Worse? Indifferent? Relaxed? Whatever it is, that is OK. With continued practice, you might be surprised how differently you begin to feel both within yourself and how you react to things outside of yourself.

If you are looking to simply practice mindfulness, if you wish to heal your physical or emotional pain, if you want to reduce stress and anxiety, if you want to perform the art of gratitude, or if you are just the curious type and you want to see how deeply you can experience the universe through opening yourself up to the present moment, then meditation is a habit you should begin.

7

COLD SHOWERS

Why would anyone want to take a cold shower?!

Well, as it turns out, there is a lot of science and testimonials that suggest cold showers, or cold therapy in general, have many physical and mental benefits. Let's jump in!

Firstly, let's acknowledge that the act of standing under freezing water does not sound appealing in the least, but once you get over the fact that you will most certainly be uncomfortable and agree to do it anyway, the sooner you will start to reap the rewards.

Secondly, let's discuss potential dangers of extreme cold exposure. According to the Centers for Disease Control and Prevention's cdc .gov website, *"When exposed to cold temperatures, your body begins to lose heat faster than it can be produced. Prolonged exposure to cold will eventually use up your body's stored energy. The result is hypothermia, or abnormally low body temperature. A body temperature that is too low affects the brain, making the victim unable to think clearly or move well. This makes hypothermia particularly dangerous because a person may not know it is happening and will not be able to do anything about it."*

With that said, please be careful if you plan on attempting cold exposure therapy and as always, consult a medical professional before beginning any form of new therapy, training or exercise, and if you have heart disease, this is one habit you might forego, as your body could have a shock reaction to the cold and lead to unwanted consequences. So, for the purpose of this section, we are going to assume that you are in the clear, and we will discuss moderate cold therapy; the kind you can get from your own shower.

What happens in your body when you deliberately expose it to cold?

- The release of adrenaline into the body

— Adrenaline triggers the body's natural flight-or-flight response. Our blood vessels contract and re-direct blood toward your heart, lungs, and muscles to prepare them for danger.
— When you deliberately increase your adrenaline levels (naturally) this can make you feel more alert, energized, and focused. Which is why a cold shower in the morning is a great way to help wake you up!

- Your circulation is improved

— The additional benefit of this adrenaline response to cold exposure [cold showers] is that it stimulates circulation within the body. By constricting the blood vessels near your skin and directing blood flow to more important areas, like your vital organs, it's like a workout for your circulatory system and promotes healthier circulation all around.

- The release of dopamine (your mood may improve)

— Dopamine is often referred to as the "feel-good" hormone. When you experience something pleasurable, your brain releases more dopamine and in turn, makes you feel *good*. Symptoms of elevated dopamine levels might be alertness, focus, more energy, motivation, and a positive mood.

— Standing under cold water doesn't seem like it would generate a pleasure producing hormone, but once you finish, the results may show differently.

- Increased metabolism

— When your body is cold, you shiver, which increases your metabolic rate. Being cold causes your body to burn more calories in order to increase core temperature. This process can kick start your metabolism.

- Your hair and skin retain their natural oils

— Showering in cold water will tighten your pores, which can help protect you from dry skin and hair by preventing your body's natural oils from being stripped away, as they often are when your pores are open during hot baths or showers.

- Your immune system may improve

— At least one study by PLoS One, published with the National Library of Medicine, showed a 29% decrease in sickness related absences from school or work.

• You may notice pain relief

— Cold tends to slow things down, such as nerve signals telling your brain how much something hurts.

— Additionally, cold is a good way to battle swelling and inflammation.

With all of these great benefits, are you ready to add cold showers to your daily habits? If so, here are some recommendations for getting started:

• Ease into it. As excited as you may be to take a plunge into an ice bath, don't shock your body or convince yourself on the first day that this isn't the thing for you. Take your time; try one or two cold showers per week. Many of the experts suggest no more than 11 total minutes of deliberate cold exposure per week, anyway.

• Try taking a standard shower at first, then end it with just a brief exposure to the cold water. If you have a waterproof watch or a smart home device that you can use to time yourself, that's great; if not, try counting to yourself or out loud. You might try as little as 5 seconds your first day or even your first week, then gradually build up tolerance. Make this a challenge, see if you can work up to a full minute. Eventually, see if you can complete your full normal shower routine in nothing but cold water.

- Set yourself a schedule and track your progress. This can be your daily routine, or you can set out 3 or 4 days per week to deliberately expose yourself to cold water.

One thing that you might discover after doing this long enough, is that your tolerance to more things than just cold water increases. The act of repeatedly exposing yourself to discomfort and learning to accept it and push through it, will pour over into other areas of your life. Small inconveniences won't appear to be so aggravating. Annoying people will appear to be less irritating. You will be able to manage pain and stress easier. You'll become tougher; more resilient; a better version of yourself.

~ And your hot water bill will go down!

8

GO OUTSIDE

Did your mother ever tell you as a kid, "Go play outside!" She may have been on to something.

In today's age of advanced technology; computers in every pocket and televisions in every room of the house, people are finding themselves inside now more than ever. The grand percentage of tech jobs, the slew of internet influencers, the army of gamers, streaming television companies providing unlimited options for binge worthy entertainment without having to thumb through a TV guide and waiting for the specific day and hour that your favorite show is aired — Why would you want to go outside?!

Because it is good for you, that's why.

In the days before the industrial age, back before our good friend Edison introduced us to the light bulb, we used the sun to tell us when it was time to get up and to go to bed. If the sun was up, you were out farming; sun down, use your candle to find your bed chamber and get some shuteye for the long day ahead. The sun helps to balance the body's circadian rhythm and regulate its production of melatonin, the hormone responsible for managing your sleep/wake cycle. Your circadian rhythm is what runs your internal clock. If this is off balance, you may experience poor sleep quality or other sleep disorders. Getting a nice dose of sunlight soon after waking in the morning, tells our internal clock that it's time to get to work. This, however, is not the only reason we need sunlight. Although proper sleep is good for your health, so is nutrition.

Vitamin D is necessary for your body to properly absorb calcium, which is required to build and maintain healthy bones, and, according to the Mayo Clinic, it also acts as an anti-inflammatory, an antioxidant, and supports immune health, muscle function, and brain cell activity, while regulating many other cellular functions in the body.

You can acquire Vitamin D naturally through certain foods, like oily fishes, mushrooms, and egg yolks, and other foods that have been fortified, and of course through the various supplements available on the market or those prescribed by your healthcare provider, but most of the Vitamin D that you receive is acquired through exposure to direct sunlight, which causes a chemical reaction that triggers the conversion process of a chemical in your skin, which leads to the creation of this essential nutrient. (We are solar powered).

Symptoms and side-effects of Vitamin D deficiency are things like, fatigue, muscle aches, depression, osteoporosis, and bone and joint pain. Vitamin D deficiency can affect anyone, regardless of age, sex, or race. According to an article by the Cleveland Clinic, approximately 35% of adults in the United States have a deficiency of Vitamin D. If you experience any of the symptoms listed above, be sure to mention it to your healthcare provider and inquire if you should be tested for low levels. In the meantime, get outside and get some rays. (15-20 Minutes of sun exposure per day is generally a good dose, but be careful not to overdo it either. Too much of a good thing can also be a bad thing. Protect yourself.)

Beyond sleep and nutrition, the mere act of being outside, whether it is on a gorgeous nature hike, a light stroll around your neighborhood, or just simply sitting on your porch and watching cars drive by, provides a sense of connection with the world; not the kind that social media and the internet provides — the kind that brings you closer to nature and life. Walk barefoot in the grass, take your kids or grandchildren to the park, visit a garden, climb a mountain, dip your toes in a pond, go fishing, skip some rocks, play a round of golf, breathe in some fresh air. It will ground you to the earth, it will promote a sense of well-being, it will fuel your soul and you will be grateful for those little moments when it's time to get back to the grind. You don't want to look back when you are older and less mobile and wish that you had gotten out of the office or house more. Go. See. Do.

9

BUILD A BUDGET

What's the old saying? — "A penny saved, is a penny earned." With inflation and the high cost of living these days, it seems nearly impossible to save even that one penny. But if that's all you can do, then most certainly do it.

If you can afford a financial advisor, then make the investment into your financial future. These are licensed professionals whose job it is to try and prepare you financially down the road. They want you to meet your financial goals, they want your investments to be safe and secure. They want you to be able to retire with a nest egg, and they made a profession out of taking care of your financial needs.

If you can't afford a financial advisor, or you would prefer to handle your own finances, or if your own finances have gotten out of hand and you need to reel them in, or if your finances are perfect and you just want to become even more savvy, or you are just curious about different ways to budget and save money — whatever your situation is, building a functional budget (and sticking to it) is never a bad idea.

Like many of the habits in this book, there is a plethora of information available on how to save money, how to retire early, how to spend less, earn more, etc. This section is just going to discuss basic concepts, and provide suggestions that have been proven to create simple ways of creating and following a budget. So let's begin with the most basic concept of all — SPEND LESS THAN YOU EARN. Of course, this is often times easier said than done, so to help you visualize and ensure that you are doing just that, below you will find steps to map out your money situation and budget for success.

First thing, we'll assume that you have both a checking and a savings account, but just in case, if you do not — open one of each, and then open a second savings account in addition (we'll get to that shortly). If for some reason you are unable to open these accounts, then acquire a safe, a money box, three shoe boxes — some way to separate your currency.

Next, grab a pen and paper, or open your favorite spreadsheet application and begin listing out all sources of your income, current assets, any recurring expenses, and all forms of debt. — We'll assume this process is for personal finances. If you have business accounts, these should be listed separately.

Beginning with your Sources of Income — You, your spouse (if combined) second job, side hustle, trust, etc. These numbers should be Net only. You can't pay bills with Gross income; only net.

Next, list out all of your Stored Assets — Checking accounts, savings accounts, investment accounts, your vehicles (if not leased/financed), any properties you own, etc.

Next, list out all of your <u>Recurring Bills</u>. (This should Not include credit cards or lines of credit) — This should be things like car insurance, internet service, phone bill, utilities, groceries, gasoline, child care, etc. DO add your two savings accounts to this list, as these will be considered recurring bills.

Finally, list out any expenses in the form of <u>Debt</u> — This would be credit cards, your mortgage, personal loans, lines of credit, student loans; anything that eventually has a payoff.

Unless you're the type of person that likes to budget down to the cent, one easy hack to ensure your checking account always has a little cushion in it is by rounding all income Down to the nearest $5, and by rounding all expenses Up to the nearest $5. This means that if you follow your budget to the 'T' then you are ensuring that you are always spending less than you are budgeted for. If things are too tight for this in the budget, try just rounding to the nearest even number then work on expanding that gap.

Once you have all of your data, subtract the total of your Expenses from your total Income. The number you see left over, combined with the total number of assets and savings you have, will give you a good determination of your financial situation. Obviously, the higher this number the better, so if it is lower than you wish to see, this is where you review your recurring bills and see if there is anywhere that you can save money. Are you paying for any subscriptions that you don't use? Would it be time to review your insurance plan and possibly shop around for a more affordable policy? Do you have a leaky toilet that is costing you extra money each month on the water/sewer bill?

When it comes to credit cards, these must be used as delicate tools.

Credit card use can easily get away from you, because you don't feel the money disappear at the time of purchase. Every bill is a surprise; especially when high interest is attached. But credit cards are also a great way to build good credit history. A good recommendation for how to use them is to assign your card to one or more recurring bill categories, such as a card specifically for gasoline and nothing more. This allows you to budget for gasoline, something you were going to spend money on anyway, and then you just use that one card for each fuel purchase and pay it with your budgeted gasoline funds. This is also a great way to keep track of how much fuel you go through each month.

The same can be done for multiple recurring bills, such as streaming services, insurance, utilities, etc. Things that you are already going to pay anyway can be budgeted and assigned to one card, then you only pay the card each month instead of the individual bills each time. Many cards have the added benefit of *cash back* or other rewards, like frequent flyer miles. As long as you don't use the card for anything else and you make your budgeted payment, your credit score grows and your pocket is no less empty. Be sure to regularly evaluate your individual bills, however, to determine if their budgeted amounts need to be adjusted.

If you are in the sticky situation that many other families are; high credit card balances have you in a tight financial spot. To climb out of this hole, you might consider contacting a credit card debt relief company. If you are not ready for that yet, and you wish to try improving your situation on your own, then consider applying for zero percent interest cards and transferring your balances (Just be sure you stop using the cards after moving the balances!) Another option that has been suggested by some financial advisors is something called the snowball method, in which you pay the minimum amount due on your highest balances and pay as much as possible on your lowest balance. When the lowest balance card is paid off, you take the extra money now freed and put it towards the next lowest balance and repeat the process until they are eventually all paid.

Be careful with credit cards. Use them wisely.

Now, with regard to having two savings accounts. The idea is that one is for goals and desires and the other is for emergencies and to be hidden from view. Budget an amount to go into each of these and never look at the hidden account. It's none of your business how much is in there. Hopefully you never need to access it, but should an emergency situation come up, you'll be glad it's there.

For the goals and desires account, this is a way for you to work towards something you want. If you desire a new television set, for example, then price it. Don't put it on credit. Price it. Set that price as a goal and do the math — How long would it take me to save up for this television? Then put it on your calendar and track your progress. The closer you get to your goal, the more exciting it becomes. And sometimes, by postponing the gratification, you discover some things. Maybe you don't actually need or desire it as much as you originally thought and you find a better use for that money. Maybe you do still want it, and by waiting you learned a bit of patience. Maybe by waiting and saving, an even better opportunity will have presented itself. And in this situation, you aren't in debt because of not waiting. Patience is a virtue after all.

Finances can be one of the biggest stressors in one's life. Take the time to evaluate your situation and make a sound plan. Budget wisely and stick to it. Know your weaknesses and take steps to prevent slipping into them. Remember to make the better choices — High dollar coffee house latte or brew a cup at home? Spend concession stand prices to see a movie at the theater or wait until it's available on video? (Or streaming these days). Eat out each day for lunch, or start packing a sack lunch? These small choices can add up little by little, and we all know that compound interest is one of the most powerful things in the universe.

10

READ

"**R**eading is essential for those who seek to rise above the ordinary." — Jim Rohn

One of the greatest gifts a person can receive is the ability to read. And one of the greatest habits a person can practice is that very same gift.

It's certainly useful, being able to read for necessity; say for work, or the instruction manual when putting together your new entertainment center, or the street signs when you're trying to get around town. But reading for pleasure, or with purpose, this is a different experience. It lights up different areas of the brain and opens up new worlds. Too often these days our imaginations are told to us, through special effects and movie magic and the story lines that are snipped and altered to fit specific narratives. We rarely have the occasion to use our own imaginations. To take the words as they are described and form our own pictures, go to interesting or fanciful places in our own minds. To glean something new from the experts, perhaps to gain a new perspective from someone else's point of view.

Books have a way of transporting the reader, of informing the reader, and of causing the reader to do something that seems to be happening less and less these days — to think.

If you're looking for one more healthy habit to include in your life, let's find out why reading should be on that list.

- Can it lower heart rate? - Check!
- Can it lower blood pressure? - Check!
- Can it reduce stress? - Check!
- Can it decrease cognitive decline - Check!

A study published in The Telegraph newspaper showed that reading for even six minutes can be enough to reduce stress levels in the body by more than two thirds. But that's not all, in a study conducted by Rush University Medical Center, they discovered that people with more frequent cognitive activity during their lives, such as reading, had slower cognitive decline. Basically, if you don't use it, you lose it!

This is likely a result of keeping the brain stimulated. There are numerous studies available that show how reading enhances focus and concentration, while also helping to improve memory, and the practice of keeping your brain active has positive effects with relation to Alzheimer's and dementia.

But let's look at some of the other benefits of reading. One of the biggest of course is gaining new knowledge. Whether you are learning about a location, a time in history, a new scientific discovery, a new language, a new skill, or even just some new material for your dad-jokes repertoire. Reading provides endless opportunities to gain information about things you didn't know before. So yeah, reading can make you smarter!

Read-ing makes you a better Read-er. The more you do something, the better you get at it. Regular reading habits will improve your ability to move through a page smoothly while being better able to retain what you've read. The practice of continuously filling your mind with repeated words, both new and already known, will also help to increase your vocabulary. This process then goes full circle, because when you are a better reader, you gain a sense of what proper or creative writing looks like, and coupled with a larger vocabulary, you may find that you become a better writer as well.

Reading is a healthy form of entertainment, and if you have a library card, it is a *free* form of entertainment. Not everything that you read must be for the purpose of learning. Let yourself be immersed inside of a great mystery, or an exciting tale of knights and dragons, or get caught up in the latest romance novel. Allow your imagination to explore and be stimulated.

Ultimately, when you have an endless supply of material to feed and stimulate your mind, protect it from age related diseases, provide free entertainment, relax you and reduce your physical and mental stress, make you smarter, build your vocabulary and writing skills, then who wouldn't want to take advantage of such a simple and rewarding activity. And with today's technology, thousands of books are at the reach of your fingertips through e-Books, downloadable instantly, or you can now listen to virtually any title on the market through audio books. Read [listen] as you commute to work, as you exercise, as you do your daily chores. Books and the knowledge and entertainment contained within them are more available to you now than they ever have been.

Take advantage of this incredible gift.

Too much of our time is spent staring down at a tiny screen watching a continuous stream of short video clips, each scientifically designed to be as long as our tiny attention spans can handle without getting bored with it. Continuous instant gratification and mind-numbing content is causing our attention spans to shrink even further and our imaginations to suffer. It's time that you replace the funny cat-videos from time to time with something that is beneficial to your brain, rather than something that is going to numb it.

Make Reading a habit.

11

Conclusion

So, here we are. Ten simple habits that you can start practicing today. Once you begin to integrate these into your life, it is sure to have a positive effect on your physical and mental well-being.

Making positive changes to your life doesn't have to be difficult. Some things require the big decisions and the struggle of climbing that hill in order to see the sun rise from the top, but often times, it's the smallest changes that can create the biggest results.

Some of this advice may already have been known to you, some a novel idea, and perhaps others just aren't your cup of tea, but if you can take away at least one or two of the habits mentioned in this book, if not all, and work them into your own routines - even tweaking them as necessary in order to fit your needs and your goals, then you are on your way to improving your life and growing as a person. And intentional personal growth is of course one of the best habits you can have.

Stay happy, stay healthy, and enjoy your journey to personal growth and improving your life !

Thanks for reading,

Resources

Cold Related Illnesses | NIOSH |CDC. (n.d.). https://www.cdc.gov/niosh/topics/coldstress/coldrelatedillnesses.html

Dopamine: What It Is, Function & Symptoms. (n.d.). Cleveland Clinic. https://my.clevelandclinic.org/health/articles/22581-dopamine

Endocrine Society. (2023, January 5). *Adrenal Hormones.* https://www.endocrine.org/patient-engagement/endocrine-library/hormones-and-endocrine-function/adrenal-hormones

Hope, B. C., McGrath, B. M., McGrath, B. M., Ducker, B. J., Sanderson, B. D., & Edwards, B. L. (2009, March 30). *Reading "can help reduce stress."* The Telegraph. https://www.telegraph.co.uk/news/health/news/5070874/Reading-can-help-reduce-stress.html

Koh, M. (2019, May 9). *The Functions of Water in the Body – Benefits of Drinking Water.* Exceed Nutrition. https://exceednutrition.com/the-functions-of-water-in-the-body/

Sissons, C. (2020, May 27). *What is the average percentage of water in the human body?* https://www.medicalnewstoday.com/articles/what-percentage-of-the-human-body-is-water

The Effect of Cold Showering on Health and Work: A Randomized Controlled

Trial. (2016, September 15). National Library of Medicine National Center for Biotechnology Information. Retrieved January 8, 2023, from https://www.ncbi.nlm.nih.gov/pmc/articles/PMC5025014/

Vitamin D. (2021a, February 9). Mayo Clinic. https://www.mayoclinic.org/drugs-supplements-vitamin-d/art-20363792

Vitamin D Deficiency: Causes, Symptoms & Treatment. (n.d.). Cleveland Clinic. https://my.clevelandclinic.org/health/diseases/15050-vitamin-d-vitamin-d-deficiency

Wergin, A. R. (2022, September 29). *Water: Essential for your body.* Mayo Clinic Health System. https://www.mayoclinichealthsystem.org/hometown-health/speaking-of-health/water-essential-to-your-body

What Is Too Much Water Intake? (2021, April 9). WebMD. https://www.webmd.com/diet/what-is-too-much-water-intake

Wilson, R. S. (2013, July 23). *Life-span cognitive activity, neuropathologic burden, and cognitive aging.* Neurology. https://n.neurology.org/content/81/4/314.short?sid=a1bfa954-8377-4c64-bb4f

About the Author

Brandon Cobb currently resides with his wife and son in Lawrenceburg, Kentucky, United States. He is a graduate of Sullivan University, with a degree in Business Management, carries a Law Enforcement Instructor's Certification from the KY Law Enforcement Council, and has graduated from the International Security Agency Academy's bodyguard school in Stockholm Sweden. Brandon has a passion for self-improvement, learning, and acquiring new skills and abilities. During the writing of this book, Brandon was studying three new languages and learned how to solve the Rubik's cube. While maintaining a career with State Government, he also created a Real Estate investment company, frequently flipped houses, acquired his black belt in Taekwondo, and is now considering raising chickens in his backyard.

~ So if this guy can do it - So can you !